IMAGES
of America

GREATER
ROLAND PARK

Having just left the stop at 4800 Roland Avenue, the No. 29 streetcar pulls out of Long Lane at the beginning of its trip to Pratt Street. The journey will take half an hour. The vehicle is a Pullman-Standard PCC, of which Baltimore ordered 27 in 1935, the second city to do so. The first PCC to be delivered to Baltimore, car No. 7023, arrived on September 2, 1936. (Courtesy of the Baltimore Streetcar Museum.)

ON THE COVER: Three motormen stand proudly on a Roland Park streetcar in about 1900. To the right is the Roland Park "business block," as the Roland Park Company called 4800 Roland Avenue. The advertisement on the front of the streetcar says, "Emory Grove Camp-Meeting Aug. 4th to 21st." Emory Grove was a Methodist retreat in Glyndon. There was a revival meeting there every summer, lasting about two weeks. (Courtesy of the Baltimore Streetcar Museum.)

IMAGES
of America

GREATER
ROLAND PARK

Douglas P. Munro

ARCADIA
PUBLISHING

Published by Arcadia Publishing
Charleston, South Carolina

Library of Congress Control Number: 2014940948

For all general information, please contact Arcadia Publishing:
Telephone 843-853-2070
Fax 843-853-0044
E-mail sales@arcadiapublishing.com
For customer service and orders:
Toll-Free 1-888-313-2665

Visit us on the Internet at www.arcadiapublishing.com

For my mother and late father

CONTENTS

Acknowledgments

Among the major institutional sources of images for this book were the Baltimore County Public Library (BCPL); the Baltimore Streetcar Museum (BSM); the Maryland State Archives' Special Collections (MSASC); and the Smithsonian Institution, Archives of American Gardens, Thomas Warren Sears Collection (SIAAG).

At the Smithsonian, Kelly Crawford supplied the Thomas Warren Sears photographs. I am indebted to Maria Day at the Maryland State Archives and to her former boss Edward C. Papenfuse for the maps at the beginning of every chapter. The Baltimore Streetcar Museum staff allowed me to browse through their photographic holdings; I would particularly like to thank the BSM's Jerry Kelly and Charlie Plantholt. The largest source of images for the book was the Baltimore County Public Library. Two library employees—Cody L. Brownson-Katz and Jason Domasky—worked tirelessly to supply well over 100 photographs. Jason's wife, Melissa Schehlein, was most helpful in assisting me in planning my approach to writing, Melissa herself being a previous Arcadia author.

As for local residents, there are too many to acknowledge individually, but a few deserve special mention. Bob and Sue Clark, Leslie Goldsmith, Jean Marvel, Tony Pinto, Barrie Sigler, and Eric Schott all allowed me unlimited access to their large collections of Roland Park–area memorabilia.

Last, but certainly not least, I would like to thank the Roland Park Community Foundation under Mary Page Michel for being so supportive of my efforts, and my wife, Cyd, for helping with proofreading.

INTRODUCTION

"Baltimore without Roland Park would be almost unthinkable." So says James F. Waesche on the first line of his 1987 book, *Crowning the Gravelly Hill*. This is not an exaggeration. Roland Park was a crucial early step in the suburbanization of metropolitan Baltimore.

Before about the late 1870s, there were virtually no suburbs. One either lived in an urban area, typically in a row house, or in the countryside—with no in-between. It is true that in the 19th century there were suburbs in the technical sense of housing just outside the city limits, but that is not the suburban lifestyle thought of today. That came with the "garden suburb," a useful term coined by Britain's early suburban developers. Garden suburbs were ideally characterized by greenery, trees, space, and a prohibition on commercial activities in all but small, designated areas.

In this sense, one can have a suburb within the city limits, as all of Roland Park now is, just as one can have a townhouse community outside the city limits that is not suburban in the sense that the early Roland Park developers thought of the term. What makes the absence of Roland Park so unthinkable is that Roland Park was the catalyst for the Baltimore suburban movement that followed it. Had Roland Park failed, the development of northern Baltimore would quite probably have been very different.

Roland Park was not Baltimore's first garden suburb, and it was certainly not the nation's. It was, however, early to incorporate the landscape into its planning. It conformed to the local topography, and not the reverse. Streets and alleys—always called "roads" and "lanes" in Roland Park—were, from the outset, laid out to obey the area's many existing hills and dales, as opposed to being superimposed over these features in the grid pattern so prevalent at the time. The West Arlington section of Baltimore was developed along suburban lines contemporaneously with Roland Park, but unlike the latter, it was platted in the traditional grid pattern. Pleasant as it may have been, it thus represented less of a deviation from the norms of the period.

More like Roland Park in terms of land use were Sudbrook Park and Mount Washington, both of which predate Roland Park. However, there were differences. Mount Washington became a community along garden-suburb lines, but more by accident than by design. It emerged from an existing small mill town, while Roland Park was conceived and built entirely from scratch. Sudbrook Park is more Roland Park–like. It was designed in 1889 by Frederick Law Olmsted Sr. of New York Central Park fame, also known as the father of the landscape architect Olmsted brothers who were so important in the laying out of Roland Park. But Sudbrook Park was considerably farther away from the city center (nine miles) than was Roland Park (four miles). It remained at 50 houses for decades, while Roland Park grew to several hundred.

One reason for this was Roland Park's other key asset. In addition to being a garden suburb, it was, unlike Sudbrook Park, what came to be known as a "streetcar suburb." In an age without automobiles, it was comparatively easy to get downtown from Roland Park. As early as 1893, the Lake Roland Elevated Railway ferried commuters from the city to Roland Park, going on to Lake Side Park, a leisure park near Lake Roland. And as of 1908, the No. 29 streetcar brought residents into Roland Park up the new and gracefully landscaped University Parkway, still one of Roland Park's treasures.

None of this happened by accident, and none of it would have happened without Edward H. Bouton, the Roland Park Company's secretary, general manager, and, later, president. (In 1891, at the time of the company's incorporation, the Kansan Bouton was a 32-year-old working for the Baltimore *Manufacturers' Record*. How he became involved with the company is unclear, but he may have been previously known to company investors R.R. Conklin and S.M. Jarvis, who were also Kansans, and Charles P. Grasty, who had a position at the *Record*.) Despite the opposition of local estate owner Charles J. Bonaparte and also of the Baltimore County commissioners, streetcars got to Roland Park. In October 1891, Bouton had the Roland Park Company's workers lay the tracks of the Lake Roland Elevated Railway along the still-unfinished Roland Avenue so as to present the county commissioners with a fait accompli. Legal maneuverings held up service for another 18 months, but the streetcars of "the El" at last arrived in Roland Park in spring 1893.

Bouton was also the driving force behind the creation of University Parkway, hitherto a muddy track called Merryman's Lane. By 1908, Bouton had overseen the company's conversion of Merryman's Lane into a grand entrance boulevard, overcoming severe topographical problems to create an avenue simultaneously naturalistic but sufficiently graded to take the tracks of the new No. 29 streetcar service.

Along with the Roland Park Company's early subsidizing of the Baltimore Country Club (to attract well-heeled golfers), the company's efforts to get efficient trolley transportation to Roland Park eventually assured its success. This led to similar developments near Roland Park. The company itself went on to new glories in the form of Guilford and Homeland to the east (not covered in this book), while other developers built northward: New North Roland Park, the Orchards (with company involvement), Poplar Hill, and, after World War II, the developments on the southern side of Lake Roland. Roland Park's triumph also guaranteed the success of what are known as the "enclave" neighborhoods, each more or less surrounded by Roland Park. (Evergreen predates Roland Park, Tuxedo Park is contemporaneous, and Keswick is newer.)

Together, all these neighborhoods form Greater Roland Park. The great majority of this area is in the city of Baltimore, for the municipal boundary was moved from a line bisecting University Parkway at the southern end of Roland Park to one bisecting Lake Avenue, about two miles north, on New Year's Day 1919. Of the area under consideration, only the Lake Roland developments are not now within the city limits—proving that a pleasant, garden-suburb lifestyle can indeed be had within urban boundaries, an important consideration for those concerned about the ever-ongoing devouring of green pastures for distant exurbs.

One

EASTERN BEGINNINGS

The area covered in this chapter comprises Roland Park's Plat 1, Embla Park to the east, and the "enclave" neighborhoods of Evergreen and Tuxedo Park. At 112 acres, Plat 1 occupies about the same area as the other three combined. Plat 1 development started in 1891.

To effect this development, the Roland Park Company of Baltimore was incorporated on July 30, 1891, and named for Roland Thornbury, an early colonial landowner in the area (he died in 1696). With Edward H. Bouton as secretary, the company pooled the assets of various Baltimore investors with those of the Lands Trust Company of London, whose funds were managed locally by Kansans R.R. Conklin and S.M. Jarvis. The Panic of 1893 resulted in the locals buying out the Londoners and the solidification of Bouton's position. He managed the company until retiring in 1935.

Plat 1 was Roland Park's earliest and most conservative plat, from a design perspective. It was laid out by the German-born George E. Kessler, who was engaged by the Roland Park Company in its earliest days on the recommendation of Conklin and Jarvis. Kessler only worked for the company through December 1891, and his efforts were later overshadowed by the Olmsted Brothers firm, which from November 1897 onward worked with the company to design Plats 2 through 6 and other, later company developments. However, apart from Plat 5, Plat 1 is the only plat on the eastern side of the Roland Avenue ridge, and the eastern side is considerably less dramatic than the western side (where most of the Olmsteds' work was done). Despite the comparatively uniform acreage he had to work with, Kessler platted a development of pleasing curvilinear streets and irregular intersections, eschewing the grid design so common elsewhere. Kessler's importance should not be overlooked. His successes in Plat 1 were what allowed the company to ascend to greater heights in later years.

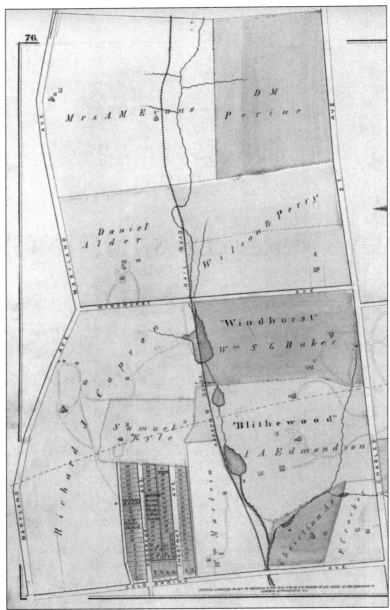

This map detail is taken from G.M. Hopkins's 1876 *City Atlas of Baltimore, Maryland, and Environs.* The map's lower left quadrant shows Richard Capron's Woodlawn estate. Capron was a director of the Roland Park Company. Along with the smaller Kyle estate, Woodlawn formed the basis of Plat 1 when development started in fall 1891. At the same time, Daniel Adler's Cherry Hill estate was sold to a separate developer, the Kansas City Land Company, which created Tuxedo Park in 1892. Just north of Adler's land, the Evans estate is now home to the Roland Park Elementary/Middle School and the Gilman School for Boys. Embla Park, occupying the southern half of the Wilson and Perry estate, was subdivided in 1898. The developed area toward the bottom of the map is West Evergreen, which dates back to 1873. The Martein estate to its immediate east was subsequently developed as Evergreen. (Courtesy of MSASC.)

This No. 24 trolley from Lake Roland has just passed the switch at the Roland Avenue business block, but it has not turned right, so it is continuing south to the Roland Water Tower. The 24 only went as far as the tower between 1940 and 1947. In the background is the Miller house, built in 1895. (Courtesy of BSM.)

This church at 4615 Roland Avenue is now North Baltimore Mennonite, but it started life as the Roland Park Methodist Episcopal in 1896. This photograph likely dates to the late 1890s. In the background are 4613 and 4611 (farthest right) Roland Avenue. The latter was originally numbered 211, the address of Roland Park developer Edward H. Bouton, before he moved to his Rusty Rocks cottage in Plat 3. (Courtesy of Tony Pinto.)

Residence, Design No. 1238

PERSPECTIVE.

In Plat 1, the Roland Park Company's earliest development, "catalog houses" are quite common. The plans could be purchased ready-made from Robert W. Shoppell's Co-operative Building Plan Association in New York, thus saving the buyer architect's fees. Catalog houses are not found in the later Roland Park plats. The particular design shown here, No. 1238 from Shoppell's 1897 catalog, is the single most common house in Plat 1. The Shoppell catalogs provided floor plans, listed construction and trim materials, and sometimes suggested paint colors. The Roland Park catalog houses are generally not absolutely true to pattern, as buyers could—and did—customize them. Modern-day owners of catalog houses that have been altered over the years find these Shoppell plans useful when looking to restore historical integrity. (Both, author's collection.)

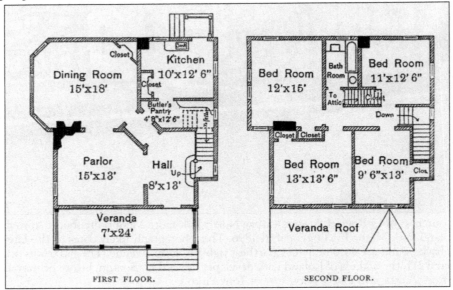

FIRST FLOOR.   SECOND FLOOR.

The intersection of Upland and Hawthorn Roads, seen here in the 1940s, is at the heart of Plat 1. The magisterial 402 Hawthorn—the McCormick house, after its first owners (of spice fame)—is immediately on the left. The fourth house on the left, 412 Hawthorn, appears to have had a tin roof in the 1940s, unusual for Roland Park, most of whose houses sported slate or cedar-shake roof shingles. (Courtesy of Tony Pinto.)

Jean A. Marvel, top left, poses with her father and bridesmaids immediately before her marriage to Geoffrey T. Keating at her home at 402 Hawthorn on June 23, 1956. Occupying two lots, 402 Hawthorn is one of the largest houses in Plat 1. The bridesmaids are, from left to right, Dorothea Marvel, Justine Kratz, and Mary Noppenberger. (Courtesy of Jean A. Keating.)

The happy couple, Jean and Geoffrey, are seen here in the side yard of 402 Hawthorn, which is actually the lot originally intended to have been 400 Hawthorn, though it was never built upon. The clergyman is the late Msgr. Thomas A. Whelan, then rector of the nearby Roman Catholic Cathedral of Mary Our Queen, built between 1954 and 1959. (Courtesy of Jean A. Keating.)

Jean and Geoffrey set off on honeymoon to Atlantic City. The car is a Chrysler DeSoto Powermaster, a model made for only a little over two years, 1952–1954. The 6,319-square-foot 402 Hawthorn is shown in all its glory in the background. Geoffrey died in 2011. The widowed Jean no longer lives in Roland Park, though her daughter is still an attorney in the area. (Courtesy of Jean A. Keating.)

The images over the next few pages are of or by various members of the Granville family, who lived at 404 Hawthorn Road at the turn of the 20th century. Many of the photographs are dated 1902. The image above shows the house itself. The photograph below shows certain family members and friends sitting on the porch steps. In the album in which these photographs were found, a handwritten caption identifies these individuals as, from left to right, (first row) "Kate, Mrs. G., 'Jo' "; (second row) "Elsie, Rosie, Mr. Granville." The album was probably Elsie's. (Both, courtesy of Barrie Sigler.)

The car is a 1901 Stanley Runabout, which had a 6.5-horsepower engine. There is no steering wheel, just a curved pole like a tiller. The Stanley Motor Carriage Company also made steam-powered cars. The period caption in the Granville album says, "Miss Haines, Dr. Rowe and Samantly," presumably the car's nickname. The photograph was taken behind 404 Hawthorn Road. (Courtesy of Barrie Sigler.)

This winter 1902 photograph shows the intersection of Upland and Hawthorn Roads, as seen from 404 Hawthorn. Beyond the intersection are 325 and 329 Hawthorn. Just visible at the left is 401 Hawthorn, thought to be first lot sold by the Roland Park Company, though not the first house built. The lot was bought in 1892 by Louis Lewis, a clothing jobber, with the house being completed in 1894. (Courtesy of Barrie Sigler.)

Another of the Granville photographs, this shot was taken from the front of 404 Hawthorn. The subjects are a Miss Haines, Robert MacDuff, and Toodles the dog. In the background on the right is Louis Lewis's 401 Hawthorn Road, while to the left is 405 Hawthorn Road, an excellent example of a Shoppell No. 1238 catalog house. This example is a reversed 1238, with the front door positioned on the left, not the right. (Courtesy of Barrie Sigler.)

Pictured here is Elsie Granville with a little girl named Ruth. The date is March 1902. In the near background is 406 Hawthorn, and beyond it, No. 412 with its early, and now long-gone, tin roof. (Courtesy of Barrie Sigler.)

In a photograph dated July 1902, this is Elsie Granville, the probable original owner of the Granville album, along with Tony the cat. The site is the front lawn of 404 Hawthorn Road. Opposite are 407 and 411 Hawthorn Road. In Roland Park, single houses built on double lots consume two house numbers, which is why the street numbering is frequently not strictly sequential. (Courtesy of Barrie Sigler.)

These photographs were taken outside 423 Hawthorn Road. Above, the flag hanging outside the house on the opposite side of the road, 509 Hawthorn Road, is a 48-star flag; this version of the flag was long lived (1912–1959) and therefore does not much help to date the images. The World War I era seems about right from the clothes. The tallest of the three "nurses" is pictured again at the center of the image below, taken at a birthday party. (Both, courtesy of Barrie Sigler/ Judy Dobbs.)

The two photographs here, and those over the next few pages, were all taken around 4824 Keswick Road (then Forest Road, and before that, Notre Dame Avenue) in the 1910s. The house was built in about 1898. The subjects are siblings Margaret W. "Mardie" Wood and H. Graham Wood. The image at left, taken in about 1915, shows the children in front of the house. The photograph below, dated May 3, 1914, was taken in the backyard, with 4826 Keswick in the background. Graham would grow up to become one of the founders, in 1952, of the Roland Park Baseball League. (Both, courtesy of Barrie Sigler.)

The image above, again of the Wood children, is the oldest of this series of Wood family photographs. The siblings appear to be about one and two years old here, probably dating the picture to 1913. In the background, across the alley, is 501 Hawthorn Road, which subsequently changed remarkably little over the ensuing century. The children are older in the image below, dating it to about 1916. They are posing with their father, a lumber company executive. The house in the background, visible between 4824 (right) and 4826 Keswick Road, is 4825 Keswick Road, which is still painted white to this day. (Both, courtesy of Barrie Sigler.)

Margaret "Mardie" Wood went to the Roland Park Country School and graduated in 1931. She married George D.F. Robinson Jr., subsequently a Maryland National Bank vice president, and the couple settled on Longwood Road. George died in 1993, and Mardie died in 2013, aged 101. Here, she is pictured in about 1917, sitting in front of 4824 Keswick, with 4826 behind. A For Sale sign is on the porch of 4826. (Courtesy of Barrie Sigler.)

H. Graham Wood attended the Gilman School, graduating in 1928. He went on to become senior vice president of the First National Bank of Maryland. Graham's first love was steamboats. He was the coauthor of *Steamboats Out of Baltimore* (1968), and served for decades as treasurer of the Steamboat Historical Society of America. This is Graham in the front yard of 4824 Keswick Road in about 1917. He died in 1998. (Courtesy of Barrie Sigler.)

This undated photograph of the Roland Park public school was taken before the addition of the first west wing, which was in place by 1929. The bus to the right has painted along its side, "United Railways and E. Co." (with "E" standing for "Electric"). United Railways and Electric (URE) was a major streetcar company in Baltimore from 1899 through 1935. URE also provided charter bus transportation. (Courtesy of Tony Pinto.)

Pictured are the 1947 ninth grade (above) and the 1962 seventh grade (below) classes at what is now the Roland Park Elementary/Middle School, then Roland Park Public School No. 233. In the picture above, the boy second from the right in the third row is John Pleier, whose photographs are extensively featured in the next chapter. In 1947, ninth grade was the highest offered by this school. From 1957, it went up through junior high, but it now goes no higher than eighth grade. Below, readers will notice the civil defense Casualty Clearing Station sign to the right of the door; this 1962 photograph was taken at the height of the Cold War. (Above, courtesy of Eric Schott; below, courtesy of Leslie Goldsmith.)

The Friends School of Baltimore moved to Greater Roland Park in 1929. Friends is Baltimore's oldest private school, dating back to 1784. The current Embla Park campus is the institution's fourth location. This 1926 photograph shows two Friends school buses outside the school's third building, 1712 Park Avenue. The sign beyond the bus on the right reads, "Park Avenue Friends Meeting." (Courtesy of BCPL.)

In 1925, Friends bought 34 acres of the Perine estate (shown as the northern half of the Wilson and Perry estate on the 1876 map at the start of this chapter). The school's Primary Department, now the Lower School, moved to the new campus in 1929, with the Intermediate Department following in 1931, and the High School in 1932. This photograph shows the construction of the Primary Department in 1927 or 1928. (Courtesy of BCPL.)

The short-lived but distinctive Shriners' Boumi Temple stood on 21 acres at the southwest corner of Charles Street and Wyndhurst Avenue. The Masonic group bought the land in 1958, with the temple being completed by 1960 for $1.5 million. The 77,000-square-foot building proved costly to maintain: $12,000 a month in utilities alone. In 1996, the Shriners sold the property to nearby Loyola University (then Loyola College). The Shriners moved out in September 1998, relocating to the White Marsh suburb. Loyola demolished the building two months later and constructed a large fitness center. These photographs were taken just before the temple was pulled down. The image above shows the front entrance from Charles Street. The image below, with a view looking south from Wyndhurst Avenue, shows the demolition company's chain-link fence already in place. (Both, courtesy of BCPL.)

John H. Pleier and his elder brother George A. lived on Evergreen's Cable Street all their lives. Shown on the map at the start of this chapter as the Martein estate, Evergreen is an enclave neighborhood in the midst of Roland Park. The Pleier family appears to have moved to Evergreen in the early 20th century. John was born in 1931 or 1932, and George, probably in 1922. The brothers attended the local public school, now the Roland Park Elementary/Middle School. This image shows John at the foot of Cable Street in about 1945. The Pleiers' house was adjacent to the tracks of the Maryland & Pennsylvania Railroad, with which John was fascinated. (Courtesy of Eric Schott.)

The view is southward from the back of the Pleiers' Cable Street property. The houses directly behind the trio in the image above are 219 and 221 Alpine Road, pictured here probably in 1914. The houses to the right are the even-numbered homes of the 4500 and 4600 blocks of Wilmslow Road, the odd-numbered side having not yet been constructed. The structure with the curved roof is the Hudson Cement and Supply Company. The female figure is probably John Pleier's mother as a young woman. The picture below shows the same view, taken by John himself in summer 1964. By this time, the lumber company lot had been taken over by the utility company. The building at the top left was constructed to be an electricity substation, though neighborhood opposition precluded its ever being used as such. (Both, courtesy of Eric Schott.)

Standing at the foot of Cable Street is the same young woman as shown on the previous page, presumably John Pleier's mother, and an unidentified little girl. The locomotive in the background is Maryland & Pennsylvania engine No. 29 or 30; both were made in 1913 by the Baldwin Locomotive Works. The photograph probably dates to 1914. The Pleiers' 207 Cable Street house is to the right. (Courtesy of Eric Schott.)

Seen from the porch of 207 Cable Street, the young woman is the same one pictured in the previous image. The man is probably her husband, the Pleier brothers' father. John's mother looks rather younger than in the previous shot. This may be the oldest of all the Cable Street photographs, perhaps dating to 1913 or so. (Courtesy of Eric Schott.)

In addition to the current BP station on Cold Spring Lane, there was a gas station opposite it, at the northwest corner of the Cold Spring and Keswick Road intersection. This photograph was taken in the 1950s by the late Paul Dorsey as part of a Lightner Photography series on service stations. The site went on to become a Video Americain movie rental store, which closed permanently in spring 2014. (Courtesy of BCPL/Lightner Photography.)

With a view looking west at the former Evergreen Methodist Protestant Church at 4622 Keswick Road, this shot was probably taken in the 1910s. The Evergreen church was long ago decommissioned and is today an attractive private house. The church's cornerstone was laid in October 1894. (Courtesy of Eric Schott.)

Two

THE RAIL BUFF'S DELIGHT

The Maryland & Pennsylvania Railroad, at least in its various early iterations, predates all development in the eastern half of Greater Roland Park—even predating West Evergreen, which, founded in 1873, is the oldest of the neighborhoods described here. (On the west side, some of the settlements along Falls Road are older.) The "Ma & Pa," as it was known, grew out of amalgamations of various small rail companies, of which the earliest were the Peach Bottom Railway between York and Red Lion, Pennsylvania, charted in 1868, and the Maryland Central Railroad between Baltimore and Bel Air, Maryland, charted in 1867. After many bankruptcies and reorganizations, these companies merged on May 5, 1891, to form the Baltimore & Lehigh Railroad. On February 12, 1901, the Baltimore & Lehigh merged with the York Southern Railroad, and the Maryland & Pennsylvania Railroad was born.

The company was never particularly profitable. Its circuitous route took 77.2 miles to cover the 49-mile distance (as the crow flies) between Baltimore and York. By the 1940s, the popularity of the automobile was severely eroding the company's profits. On May 4, 1947, Sunday passenger service was ended. Passenger service on weekdays was cut to one train per day in each direction on October 1, 1951, and on August 31, 1954, was discontinued altogether. To the dismay of many, all steam engines were put out to pasture in November 1956, leaving only diesels for locomotion. The company had a last gasp in the mid-1950s, when it was used to transport limestone to Baltimore for the construction of the Cathedral of Mary Our Queen, just east of Roland Park. When this job was complete, there was little reason for the company to retain its Maryland operation. Accordingly, on June 11, 1958, the Ma & Pa's Maryland section was wound up, with the rails being torn up for salvage shortly thereafter. The remainder of the Ma & Pa was bought by Emons Industries in 1971.

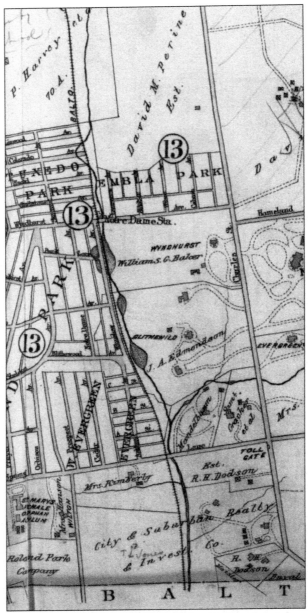

This detail is taken from the 1898 George W. and Walter S. Bromley *Atlas of Baltimore County, Maryland*, as is the one on the opposite page. Between them, the map excerpts show the route of the Maryland & Pennsylvania Railroad through Greater Roland Park. At the lower edge of this map is the 1888 city boundary, which endured until New Year's Day 1919, when the city annexed considerable amounts of land in all directions, including Roland Park. The small Roland Park Company tract at the lower left of the map, plus the City & Suburban Realty and Investment Company's land to its right (east), formed the basis of Roland Park's Plat 5 a decade later. The Kimberly estate above became the Keswick neighborhood. The three ponds that used to lie alongside the Ma & Pa tracks are now gone. Notre Dame Station is now the Wyndhurst Station shopping center. (Courtesy of MSASC.)

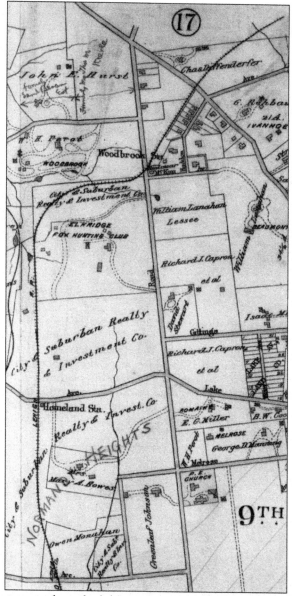

This is the continuation northward of the map on the previous page. The horizontal road at the bottom is now Northern Parkway, in 1898 a minor, unpaved road called Belvedere Avenue, which did not extend east of Charles Street. The Protestant Episcopal church above and to its right is the Church of the Redeemer. The Ma & Pa Homeland Station on Lake Avenue is now a private home. The Elkridge Fox Hunting Club was, in 1898, fairly new at this location, having leased its land from the estate of former governor Augustus W. Bradford in 1888 before buying most of it in 1892. In 1895, the club converted the land into a nine-hole golf course. This course operated next to the Baltimore Golf Club's nine-hole course, situated immediately south on land leased from the City & Suburban Realty and Investment Company. The clubs combined in 1899, emerging eventually as today's Elkridge Club. Just northeast of the club is the Ma & Pa's Woodbrook Station, now an Exxon service center. (Courtesy of MSASC.)

The Maryland & Pennsylvania Railroad was formed in 1901 as the result of a merger between the Baltimore & Lehigh and the York Southern. The Baltimore terminus was this E. Francis Baldwin building on Oak Street, at what is now the angle between the North Avenue and Howard Street bridges (the latter did not exist until 1938). The image above shows the front entrance to the station in the late 1890s. Passengers descended to the train platforms at the bottom of the Jones Falls valley via the side stairways. The tunnel in the background is the Howard Street tunnel, opened in 1895. For the image below (1905), the photographer was standing above the tunnel, looking back at the station. To the left of the station is the North Avenue bridge. The station was demolished in 1937. (Both, courtesy of BCPL.)

This 1951 photograph shows a Ma & Pa engine puffing northward through Wyman Park, about to pass under the University Parkway viaduct (built in 1908). The locomotive is engine No. 41, a low-geared switcher built by Baldwin in 1914. It is hauling cars up the steep gradient from North Howard Street (previously Oak Street) through Roland Park to the Homeland Station on Lake Avenue, at which point another locomotive may take over. After the 1937 demolition of the Oak Street station to make way for the Howard Street bridge, a small building under the North Avenue and North Howard Street bridges served as the station. (Courtesy of BCPL.)

The photographer peered over the north side of the University Parkway viaduct to snap this Ma & Pa derailment. The back of the print has "1940–50s" scrawled on it. The diesel locomotive at the top right is engine No. 81, built in 1946. At left is the Ma & Pa's X1 steam crane, built in 1899 by Industrial Works and bought refurbished by the Ma & Pa in 1928. (Courtesy of Eric Schott.)

Evergreen resident John Pleier took this photograph in the mid-1950s. His vantage point was about 110 yards north of Cold Spring Lane, looking south. The sidings on the right were for wagons delivering coal to the Evergreen coal depot, whose office was located where the disused Bank of America building currently stands and whose yard was where the Royal Farms store now is. The depot office is the dark building—a glorified shed—in the distance on the far right, beyond the grassy embankment. The first siding to the right was known as track A, and the second, just discernible, as track B. Though not visible here, track B1 split from track B even farther to the right. (Courtesy of Eric Schott.)

The locomotive is crossing the switch for the sidings to the Evergreen coal depot. At times, there were as many as five sidings in this vicinity, all running west of the main line and identified as A, B, B1, C, and D. The siding visible leading to the right is track A, from which B then split farther to the right. Over to the right again, the short B1 split from B. All three sidings served the Evergreen coal depot. Tracks C and D separated from the main line 150 yards farther north. They ran across what is now the Evergreen meadow to supply the lumber and building-supply companies at the south end. This engine is diesel No. 80. The Ma & Pa bought a total of eight diesels from 1946 to 1953. Engine 80 was sold to Republic Steel in November 1959. (Courtesy of Eric Schott.)

This is the Evergreen coal yard in January 1940, today's Royal Farms store. The coal wagon on the right is on siding B1, which terminated in a coal trestle. A trestle was an elevated length of track resting on what was, in effect, a bridge without a solid span. The coal cars stopped above the open-bottomed span and opened their bases, whereupon the coal fell though the trestle into the yard. (Courtesy of BCPL.)

The Ma & Pa ceased running in Baltimore in 1958, and post-railroad erosion, followed by streambed engineering in 2006, has left this scene changed but recognizable. The setting is Stony Run, just north of its confluence with the Homeland stream. The photograph must be post 1928, the year the Ma & Pa bought No. 62, the second of its self-propelled Electro-Motive Company gas-electric "doodlebug" cars, retired in 1955. (Author's collection.)

Evergreen resident John Pleier photographed this view from his Cable Street house. Engine 42 is pushing empty wagons northward. Engines 41 and 42 were bought by the Ma & Pa in 1914, and Engine 42 was in 1929 given a feedwater heater, which No. 41 never had. The heater is the horizontal cylinder visible in this shot just behind the headlight. Locomotive 42 was retired in 1952. (Courtesy of Eric Schott.)

This northward-steaming train has just passed Blythewood Lake, probably in the late 1890s. The fence on the right ran parallel to and about 40 yards north of what is now Oakdale Road, which then did not then exist. The photograph shows the Baltimore & Lehigh's engine No. 6, a narrow-gauge Pittsburgh Locomotive and Car Works locomotive built in 1883. It continued in service until the line was converted to standard gauge in 1900. (Courtesy of Tony Pinto.)

This is the Ma & Pa's crossing at Belvedere Avenue, now Northern Parkway. The building is the Chesapeake and Potomac (C&P) Telephone Company's "Tuxedo" exchange, now an administrative building for the Bryn Mawr School. The picture was taken in 1959 by the Baltimore Gas and Electric Company, a year after the closing of the Ma & Pa's Maryland operation. (Courtesy of BCPL/Steve Corfidi.)

This shot was probably taken immediately southwest of the Bryn Mawr School campus, where the Ma & Pa track curved slightly westward (in other words, a little to the north of the C&P building that is the subject of the previous photograph). James Gallagher took this shot, with a view looking south, in 1952 or 1954. The locomotive is engine No. 29. (Courtesy of BCPL.)

Ma & Pa locomotive 28 has just crossed Charles Street, steaming northeast toward Towson. The station is the Woodbrook Station, built in 1908 and demolished in 1954. The photograph was taken by Charles Mahan on September 29, 1951. At this point, this section of the railroad had only eight years left. The Maryland end of the line was closed on June 11, 1958, with only the Pennsylvania operation continuing thereafter. (Courtesy of BCPL.)

The northeast-looking view in the photograph above shows the Woodbrook Ma & Pa Station on Charles Street in February 1936. The tracks passed along a right-of-way still extant behind today's Eddie's Supermarket. The Bellona Avenue overpass in the distance no longer exists, and the railroad cut it used to span has been filled in and built upon. The image below shows the same scene in 1959, a year after the Ma & Pa tracks were torn up. The tracks shown in the photograph above had previously passed northeast through where the tire rack is in the image below. Nowadays at this spot on Charles Street, track remains can be seen when the asphalt is sufficiently worn. This Amoco station is now Woodbrook Exxon. (Above, courtesy of BCPL; below, courtesy of BCPL/Lightner Photography.)

Three

WESTWARD HO

Despite initially struggling lot sales in Plat 1, the Roland Park Company looked west with a view to the development of the land between Roland Avenue and Falls Road. This acreage was considerably more difficult to develop than the gently rolling Plat 1, for it was characterized by steep east/west ridges and ravines, features absent on the eastern side of Roland Avenue. To bring about the transformation of the rough land into an attractive and saleable suburb, company president Edward Bouton secured the services of the Olmsted brothers, noted landscape architects of the day. The Olmsteds—John Charles and Frederick Law Jr.— were not in fact natural brothers. Frederick (born in 1870) was the biological son of Frederick Law Sr., the famed architect of New York's Central Park. John (born in 1852) was Frederick Sr.'s nephew and, subsequently, adopted son.

John Olmsted made his first visit to Roland Park in November 1897. Conforming to Bouton's desire that Plats 2 and 3 appeal to a wealthier clientele than Plat 1 had been marketed to, lot sizes were increased substantially. In Plat 1, the standard lot size had been 50 feet of frontage by 165 feet of depth, about a fifth of an acre (though buyers quite often bought double lots). Plats 2 and 3's lots would have 75 feet of frontage and would be of more irregular shape than those in Plat 1.

The Olmsteds' signature achievement on the western side of Roland Avenue was their treatment of three ridges, now St. John's, Midvale, and Longwood Roads in Plat 3. At their western extremities, the ridges were too steep to be connected by road to anything. Consequently, the Olmsteds had vehicular traffic on each stop at a turning circle, while pedestrian traffic could continue along quite steep but paved and attractively designed footpaths. The paths survive still and are among Roland Park's most pleasing attributes.

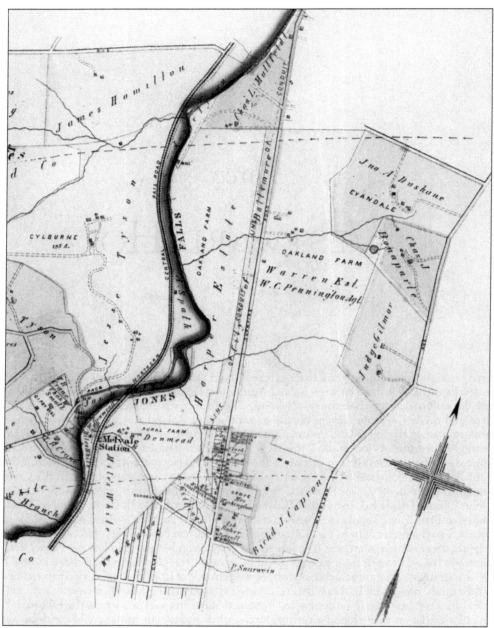

Plat 2 was the Roland Park Company's second development; its planning started in 1897. As shown here on the Hopkins 1876 *City Atlas*, the land was provided by Richard Capron, whose holdings east of Roland Avenue had made up the bulk of Plat 1. In the late 1890s, Plat 1, mostly east of Roland Avenue, was simply known as Roland Park, and what was to become Plat 2 was initially intended by the Roland Park Company to be a wholly separate—and higher-end—development with the tentative name of Braehurst. In January 1900, however, the company opted for the simple Roland Park Plat Two. This was in good measure because the early struggling sales in Plat 1 had just taken off, and the company wanted the new development to be popularly associated with the suddenly fashionable Plat 1. (Courtesy of MSASC.)

The Roland Park Woman's Club building sits on the northwest corner of the three-way intersection of Roland Avenue, Cold Spring Lane, and Ridgewood Road. The clubhouse was erected sometime between 1901 and 1904, the club itself having been founded in 1898. This photograph by Thomas Warren Sears is post 1904, but predates the addition of the clubhouse's south wing in the 1920s. (Courtesy of SIAAG.)

The building on the left is the Roland Park Country School's second location, 4608 Roland Avenue. Initially called the Roland Park School, the then coed institution was established in 1894, sponsored by the Roland Park Company. It moved to this building, then numbered 210 Roland Avenue, in 1905. The house was designed by Ernest A. Wolf III and was built in 1891. (Courtesy of Tony Pinto.)

Not much is known about this photograph of 104 Ridgewood Road. It is "part of the package" when one buys this property, being passed down from owner to owner. The photographer and the date are both unknown, but given that a part of 106 Ridgewood is visible at the right of the picture, it must have been taken before 106's demolition in 1937. (Courtesy of Jon Lewin.)

Thomas Warren Sears took this photograph of 106 Ridgewood Road in the 1910s. Deeded by the Roland Park Company to Elizabeth King Ellicott on June 24, 1901, this house was designed by her architect husband, William M. Ellicott. In 1937, Gideon N. Stieff, who lived at 108 Ridgewood Road, became concerned that 106 was about to be turned into a nursing home. He bought 106, demolished it, and incorporated its lot into his own. (Courtesy of SIAAG.)

RIDGEWOOD ROAD LOOKING NORTH TO KENWOOD.   ROWLAND PARK, MD.

This postcard view is north up Ridgewood Road. The card has no publication date, but the postmark is 1908. The house on the right is 112 Ridgewood. The houses on the even-numbered side of Ridgewood Road command an excellent view down into the Jones Falls valley to the west. (Author's collection.)

This January 1902 photograph was taken from a point 100 or so yards north of the previous image, with the view looking southward at 107 and 109 Ridgewood. The magnificent, and now long-gone, 106 Ridgewood is prominent in the distance. The car in the left foreground also appears in chapter one, in the section about the Granville family. (Courtesy of Barrie Sigler.)

The Symington brothers, Stuart and Thomas, whose home 218 Ridgewood Road once was, were the developers of Gibson Island, summer retreat of the well-to-do. On the advice of Roland Park Company president Edward H. Bouton, the Symingtons hired Olmsted Brothers, landscape architects, to plan the island. At the northern end of Ridgewood Road, No. 218 was tragically burned in 2007. The image is an early-1900s Thomas Warren Sears photograph. (Courtesy of SIAAG.)

Roland Park Residence Baltimore, Md.

This is Rusty Rocks, the beloved home of Roland Park Company president Edward Bouton. The house, between Boulder Lane and Goodwood Gardens, was built in 1907 on the site of a disused quarry, the lot being, in Bouton's view, unsuitable for sale. Rusty Rocks was designed by the Olmsted brothers and bears all the hallmarks of the rusticity they favored. (Courtesy of Leslie Goldsmith.)

Shown here in the 1910s, Nos. 200 (above) and 204 Goodwood Gardens are at the southern end of this famed block. Goodwood Gardens was the Roland Park Company's second successful attempt at a themed mini-development within the larger overall suburb, Club Road having been the first. (An early effort at something similar at the southern end of Ridgewood Road had foundered on the Olmsted landscape architects' objections and was never fully executed.) The Goodwood project was the brainchild of architect and landscape designer Charles A. Platt, though he ended up designing only one of the houses. Goodwood Gardens was and remains Roland Park's most extravagant and formal block. No. 200 was once home to Anna M.L. Corkran, president of the Women's Civic League of Baltimore. Her son was B. Warren Corkran, the golfer. (Both, courtesy of SIAAG.)

These postcards show 206 Goodwood Gardens (above) and the view north from one of its upper windows. The house was home to Daniel Willard, president of the Baltimore & Ohio Railroad from 1910 to 1941. The postcard above is postmarked June 23, 1910, while the undated one below is of the same era. The white house in the middle distance below is 211 Goodwood Gardens. The image above shows particularly well Roland Park's early road surfacing: dirt and gravel, oiled and compacted. Asphalt paving did not come to Roland Park until after its 1919 annexation by the City of Baltimore. (Both, courtesy of Leslie Goldsmith.)

These c. 1910 Thomas Warren Sears images show 209 (above) and 210 Goodwood Gardens. Born in 1880 in Brookline, Massachusetts, Sears was a prominent landscape architect, graduating in 1906 from Harvard's Lawrence Scientific School. At some point between graduation in 1906 and setting up his own practice in Philadelphia in 1913, Sears worked a couple of years for Olmsted Brothers. The well-known Olmsteds were deeply involved with the Roland Park Company in the early part of the 20th century. These, and the other Sears photographs in this book, were probably all taken during Sears's employment with the Olmsteds. (Both, courtesy of SIAAG.)

This c. 1910 postcard shows the view south from the upper floor of 210 Goodwood Gardens, the J.E. Heinrich house. No. 209 is on the left, on the opposite side of the road, while No. 205 sits in the middle of the image. The lot between 205 and 209, originally intended for No. 207, was never built upon. It forms part of the large garden of No. 205. (Author's collection.)

This Thomas Warren Sears photograph shows 211 Goodwood Gardens. The Goodwood Gardens project was architect Charles A. Platt's idea, but Goodwood's large and elaborate houses were nearly all designed by Ellicott and Emmert (designers of St. David's Church), Parker and Thomas (the Belvedere Hotel), or Edward L. Palmer Jr., the Roland Park Company's in-house architect. (Courtesy of SIAAG.)

Club Road was the Roland Park Company's first successful attempt at creating a community within a community—later ones being Goodwood Gardens, Edgevale Park, and Merryman Court. When taking this image, photographer Thomas Warren Sears was looking west toward the Baltimore Country Club, whose walled entrance the horse and buggy in the distance have just passed. The country club was the centerpiece of the Club Road mini-development. (Courtesy of SIAAG.)

Starting on Roland Avenue and extending west to the Baltimore Country Club's clubhouse, many of the houses along Club Road are built in the half-timbered Tudor style, like No. 3, shown here in this Thomas Warren Sears photograph. A lot of these houses were designed by the Wyatt & Nolting architectural firm. J.B. Noel Wyatt himself lived at 5 Club Road. (Courtesy of SIAAG.)

In a departure from standard Roland Park Company practice, the Club Road houses' gardens are walled and fenced off from the road. The idea was to attract high-income, privacy-valuing country club members. Beyond the wall and fence to the left lies 10 Club Road, which in 1927 became the home of the now-defunct Girls' Latin School. On the right is the wall behind which lies the Baltimore Country Club. (Courtesy of SIAAG.)

This 1902 photograph shows the country club's clubhouse from the north, with Club Road on the left behind the trellis. Organized in 1898, the club created a presence that was useful to the Roland Park Company. Everyone coming to play golf at the club had to come by streetcar along Roland Avenue, thereby passing some of Roland Park's grandest houses, each an advertisement for the company's wares. (Courtesy of Barrie Sigler.)

The 1896 Roland Park Golf Club was reorganized as the Baltimore Country Club in 1898. The Roland Park Company took a gamble and in some respects bankrolled the conversion of the modest golf club into the prestigious country club, hoping to attract wealthy residents. The Roland Park Company built the first clubhouse and leased it, and the land for the golf course, to the club at modest rates. Even the eventual sale of the course's land to the club resulted in no direct profit to the company. The photograph above, taken in January 1902, shows the clubhouse from quite near the first tee. This is one of very few images to show the clubhouse before the addition of its iconic semicircular veranda, shown below on an early-1920s postcard. (Above, courtesy of Barrie Sigler; below, author's collection.)

BALTIMORE COUNTRY CLUB, ROLAND PARK, BALTIMORE, MD.

This photograph almost certainly depicts the scene at the beginning of a match held at the Baltimore Country Club on April 29, 1928, featuring B. Warren Corkran and Roland MacKenzie versus Bobby Jones and Watts Gunn—all famous amateur golfers. The purpose was to raise money for the 1928 Olympic Games. Spectators are running from the first tee down toward the first green. (Courtesy of Tony Pinto.)

Designed by the local architectural firm Wyatt & Nolting, the first clubhouse was in keeping with early Roland Park styles. It was, however, fire prone, suffering damage in 1905, 1912, and 1930. On January 5, 1931, a devastating fire, shown here, burned the structure to the ground. A Federal-style masonry replacement building, constructed on the same site, was opened in 1933. (Courtesy of Tony Pinto.)

The Baltimore Country Club's course, of which little remains, spanned both sides of Falls Road. The 1st, 17th, and 18th fairways lay on the eastern side of the road, with everything else being to the west. The man at left in this 1898 image is at the second tee, with Falls Road behind him. The mound ahead is a berm covering a conduit carrying water from Lake Roland to Hampden. (Courtesy of BCPL.)

GOLF GROUNDS, BALTIMORE COUNTRY CLUB, ROLAND PARK.

The photographer is looking south from near the country club's 10th green. Today, the Village of Cross Keys shopping center is located about where the lone tree stands in the middle of the image. The hillock in the distance toward the right, leveled in the 1960s, is now the site of the Baltimore Polytechnic Institute high school. The date of this postcard is unknown. (Author's collection.)

These two images show the inner courtyard of what is now the Roland Park Condominium on Upland Road. Originally the Roland Park Apartments, this Beaux-Arts structure was designed by the Roland Park Company's Edward L. Palmer Jr. in 1925. Not shown here, the condominium's current parking garage was formerly Roland Park's communal stable, built in 1903 by Wyatt & Nolting. These 1926 photographs were taken by Frances Benjamin Johnston, known as "Fannie," a pioneering female photojournalist. Born in West Virginia in 1864, Johnston was introduced to photography by her mother, Frances Antoinette Johnston, the official White House photographer at the turn of the 19th century. Fannie died in 1952. (Both, courtesy of Library of Congress.)

With the Roland Park Apartments on the left and the Upland Road carbarn on the right, both images show the carbarn's yard. The image above was shot by C.W. White on May 31, 1940, and shows streetcars and a No. 10 trackless trolley. It is not clear why this regular-type trackless trolley is present, or even how it got here. Six weeks earlier, on April 13, the No. 10 line from downtown to Roland Park had converted to trackless. The Roland Park Civic League became alarmed at the prospect of proliferating overhead power lines and had the Public Service Commission prohibit trackless trolleys north of the water tower at Roland Park's southern boundary. For the trackless to be here, it must have been towed, there being no trackless-trolley wires north of the tower. The photograph below is about the same age. (Both, courtesy of BSM.)

People sometimes subconsciously assume that the past was static, that a historical scene shown in a photograph was somehow always that way until altered in very recent times. This, of course, is not the case, as illustrated by these two views of the Roland Park Upland Road car house. The c. 1905 image above shows the car house as it originally was, while the photograph below shows the structure shortly before its demolition. The car house's last day of operation was April 20, 1946, and the fence across the entrance shows that the later image was taken after that. In 1947, the property was bought by Robert L. Jackson, who demolished it and, in 1949, built and opened the still-extant Park Lin apartment complex on the site. (Both, courtesy of BSM.)

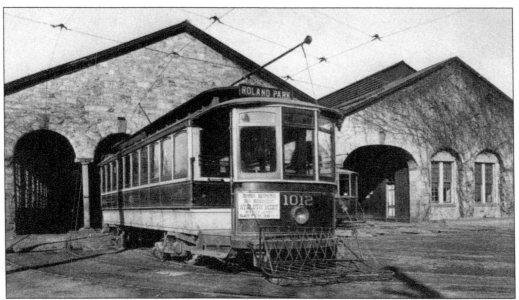

These 1902 photographs show two Brill streetcars outside the Upland Road car house (above) and the next-door Roland Park firehouse (below). Begun in 1868, the Philadelphia J.G. Brill Company was, at one point, the largest manufacturer of streetcars and buses in the world. It merged with the American Car and Foundry Company in 1944 and went out of business in 1954, having manufactured more than 45,000 public-transit vehicles. The sign on the front of the car above reads, "Johns Hopkins 5th Regiment Athletic Meet. 5th Regt. Armory. Sat. Feb. 20, 8 a.m." The 1876-founded Hopkins was still at this time housed at its cramped Mount Vernon, Baltimore, campus, with poor athletic facilities—hence the need to hold meets at the Armory at Hoffman and Howard Streets. (Both, courtesy of BSM.)

The image above shows No. 10 and No. 29 streetcars, photographed at the Upland Road car house on May 30, 1940. Below is the interior of the car house during the same era. Of the No. 10 and No. 29 lines, the 10 was considerably older, having commenced in 1893 as an electrified line between Roland Park and Point Breeze. The No. 10 came to Roland Park through Hampden to the south. In 1903, Roland Park Company president Edward Bouton hit on the notion of bypassing Hampden by converting the hitherto insignificant Merryman's Lane into a magnificent southern-entry boulevard. By 1908, having surmounted a number of topographical problems, Bouton had his boulevard, University Parkway. The No. 29 trolley route, opened on October 8, 1908, ran along its broad, lush median strip. (Both, courtesy of BSM.)

A trolley is leaving the car-house yard on April 7, 1939. The note on the back of this print reads, "This picture was taken from a No. 24 car." The 24 Lakeside line, a two-mile line between the car house and Lake Roland, was the third of the trio that served Roland Park. The line was given various numbers but is best known as the No. 24, its final designation, assigned in 1929. (Courtesy of BSM.)

A No. 29 streetcar leaves Roland Park for downtown, turning left into Long Lane behind the Roland Avenue shopping center. While the streetcars were maintained at the Upland Road car house, the actual passenger stop, shown here, was immediately west of the nearby shopping block, 4800 Roland Avenue. Streetcars entered from Roland Avenue and exited by turning south onto Long Lane, then east onto Upland Road to get back to Roland Avenue. (Courtesy of BSM.)

These two photographs give an excellent sense of the Roland Park trolley stop. The above shot dates to about 1905. The covered shelter was built fairly shortly after the 1893–1894 construction of the shopping center beyond. The image below is undated but can be placed in a narrow window. The sign reads (pointing to the right), "To Number 10 Cars" and (to the left), "To Number 28—Lakeside Cars." Subsequently the No. 24 line, the Lakeside route was called the 28 line between October 1924 and 1929. However, the second car on the left is a Peter Witt car, acquired in 1930, so the sign is uncorrected from the previous year. (Both, courtesy of BSM.)

This 1903 photograph shows trolley crewmen and two unidentified boys at the Roland Park stop. This is a reversible-seat, open-sided car, for use in summer. The backs of the benches are hinged so that they can swing over the top of the bench to serve as a back over either the front or rear lip of the bench. This permitted passengers to face forward whichever direction the car was going. (Courtesy of BSM.)

Plat 1, block 21 was reserved for commercial use by the Roland Park Company in 1891 and was always referred to by the company as the "business block." It was the only block in Roland Park proper where commercial activities were permitted, and this is still the case. The company's own office was in this building, which was designed by Wyatt & Nolting. Construction started in December 1893. This image dates to the 1920s. (Author's collection.)

Taken about a year apart, this pair of photographs shows the Upland Road car house in its final days (above) and the construction of the building that replaced it (below). The earlier image shows the business block and, beyond it, the car house. It was probably taken in the winter of 1947–1948. (The snow covering the streetcar tracks demonstrates that this image postdates Roland Park streetcar service.) In 1947, the car house was bought by Robert L. Jackson, who demolished it and constructed the Park Lin apartment complex. The image below, taken on January 7, 1949, shows the apartment building nearing completion. The west (left) wing is where the car-house yard once was. The business block is to the right. (Above, courtesy of BSM; below, courtesy of Joan Jackson.)

This photograph is of 6 Beechdale Road. The date and photographer are unknown. However, in this image, the house next door, 4 Beechdale, has already lost the porch it was originally built with—this removal probably happened in August 1928. (Courtesy of Tony Pinto.)

Here is a rear view of 104 St. John's Road, taken on March 12, 1913. St. John's Road is one of the Plat 3 roads that the Roland Park Company and Olmsted Brothers ingeniously designed to run along the tops of three steep east/west ridges whose leveling would have been cost prohibitive. The others are adjacent Midvale and Longwood Roads, the latter being the most dramatic of the three. (Courtesy of Ellen Webb.)

This is the view eastward from the end of Midvale Road in about 1910. The sign toward the right reads, "Squirrel Path." Squirrel Path is one of 18 footpaths in Roland Park, mostly in Plat 3. The Olmsted brothers were enthusiastic about the paths as a means of encouraging gentle outdoor exercise and, more practically, as a way to create pedestrian shortcuts across ravines too steep for roads. (Courtesy of Tony Pinto.)

This is what 8 Longwood Road looked like in April 1910, when John W. and Helen Doll Tottle rented it shortly before their 1912 move to New North Roland Park. A generation later, in 1946, John and Elizabeth Scott (née Tottle) bought it—not knowing that Elizabeth's parents had once lived there. The house is now owned by Elizabeth's niece and her husband. (Courtesy of Barrie Sigler.)

The Tottles had several children—John Jr., Helen, Anna Doll, Florence, and Elizabeth; John Jr. and Helen are shown here on April 25, 1910, in the backyard of 8 Longwood Road. The road to the north in the background is Deepdene Road, visible in this image because the houses that now line its south side had not yet been built. (Courtesy of Barrie Sigler.)

This spring 1911 photograph shows Helen Tottle with baby Florence (born November 23, 1910), looking northeast across the back porch of 6 Longwood Road toward Roland Avenue. The pale house in the distance is 5201 Roland Avenue, demolished in the early 1970s to make way for the current bank building, which was erected in 1974. (Courtesy of Barrie Sigler.)

Gymnasium   Girls' Latin School   Roland Park   Baltimore, Md.

The photographer of this undated postcard is looking north at the Girls' Latin School gymnasium. Located at 2 Tower Lane, the gymnasium was built in 1929 on the site of Roland Park's first water tower. The now-defunct Girls' Latin was on nearby Club Road from 1927. (Courtesy of Leslie Goldsmith.)

Roland Park Branch of Pratt Library   Baltimore, Md.

The Roland Park branch of the Enoch Pratt Free Library is shown here on this late-1920s postcard. The library stands at Roland Avenue and Longwood Road. From 2006 to 2007, the library was closed, renovated, and greatly expanded, largely as the result of community fundraising. It reopened with some fanfare on January 19, 2008. (Author's collection.)

Four

THE GRAND
THOROUGHFARE

Roland Park's main artery, the tree-lined Roland Avenue is one of the neighborhood's defining features. Once a country route called Maryland Avenue, Roland Avenue was greatly widened by the Roland Park Company in the early 1890s. By the mid-1910s, the avenue had been improved as far as Lake Avenue, thought it extended no farther than this for several decades. Not until the development of the Elkridge Apartments in the 1960s was the avenue taken farther north, along the former No. 24 streetcar right-of-way.

The streetcar was always central to the Roland Avenue project. The avenue was designed with a wide median strip upon which sat the tracks of the Lake Roland Elevated Railway, later the No. 10 streetcar line. The "El," as it was known, was a major selling point for Roland Park boosters; without it, park residents would have been faced with a daunting hour-long horse-and-buggy ride to downtown. El service to Roland Park, from downtown through Hampden, commenced in spring 1893.

After the Roland Park Company's conversion of Merryman's Lane into University Parkway, further trolley service was added. In October 1908, the No. 29 streetcar service to Roland Park began. Running along rails laid on the parkway's median, the No. 29 joined the existing No. 10 line at the intersection of University Parkway and Roland Avenue.

The other of the Roland Avenue streetcar triumvirate was the No. 24 line. In the early 20th century, the route functioned as an unnamed jerkwater (minor) extension of the No. 10 line. It operated in good measure to ferry people to Lake Side Park, a leisure park near Lake Roland that closed in 1909. The line was named the No. 11 route in 1923, though this was changed to No. 28 a year later. It finally became the No. 24 in 1929. Never a long route, it operated for most of its history between the Upland Road car house and the Lakeside terminus. From 1940 to 1947, its route was extended as far south as the Roland Water Tower. From 1947 to 1950, it ran solely north of Lake Avenue.

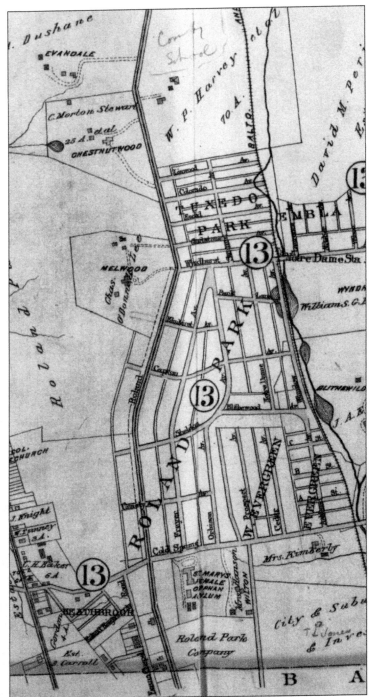

This map is a detail from the 1898 Bromley *Atlas of Baltimore County*. It shows Roland Avenue from the 1888 city/county boundary to a point just south of Belvedere Avenue, now Northern Parkway. The Plat 1 roads still have their early monikers here, with some being named after Roland Park Company investors: Capron, Fryer, and Grasty. (Courtesy of MSASC.)

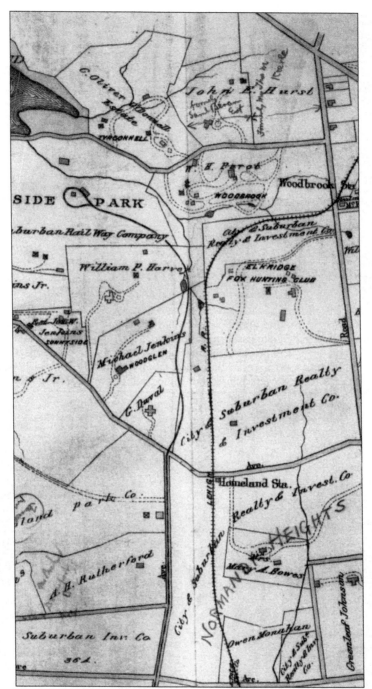

Another detail from the 1898 Bromley atlas, this shows Roland Avenue from Belvedere Avenue north to its then termination on Lake Avenue, with the streetcar line continuing to a turning loop near Lake Roland. Alexander H. Rutherford, whose estate is shown toward the bottom left of the map, was a Roland Park Company investor, though his estate was not within the boundaries of Roland Park proper. (Courtesy of MSASC.)

Seen looking north from Roland and Cold Spring, the vehicle in the middle is a combination electric trackless trolley and regular gasoline bus (the only such combination vehicle in Baltimore). The logo on its front, "BTCo," stands for the Baltimore Transit Company. This was the company that provided public transportation in Baltimore from 1935. After its mid-1940s purchase by National City Lines, streetcars were phased out in favor of buses. (Courtesy of BSM.)

This photograph dates to 1910 or so. The house farthest to the left is 4608 Roland Avenue, which had recently been occupied by the Roland Park Country School when photographed by Thomas Warren Sears. Throughout Roland Park proper, along Roland Avenue, the trolley tracks were always shielded from public view by privet hedges. (Courtesy of SIAAG.)

The photographer is looking south at the grade crossing at Roland Avenue and Oakdale Road. The sign reads, "Danger. Go Slow." This photograph was taken on July 23, 1915, by S.A. Douglas for the Maryland State Roads Commission. (Courtesy of Tony Pinto.)

This southbound No. 24 trolley is between Upland and Club Roads. The break in the hedge and posts is for the Club Road grade crossing. With a No. 24 trolley this far down Roland Avenue (that is, south of the Upland Road car house), the image must have been taken between 1940 and 1947. (Courtesy of BSM.)

This is the Roland Avenue view northward from Deepdene Road. The vacant areas to right and left are now occupied by three schools. The prominent retaining wall is still there. Alfred Waldeck took this photograph in 1916 for the Baltimore County Administrative Office. (Courtesy of BCPL.)

The photographer (the same Alfred Waldeck who took the previous photograph) is now a half mile to the north in New North Roland Park, still in 1916. The crossing in the foreground is Lehr Lane, now called St. George's Road. The ornamental hedge visible through the trees on the right marks the southern boundary of 5607 Roland Avenue, built in 1895. (Courtesy of BCPL.)

In this 1916 Alfred Waldeck image, the middle-distance crossing and left turn mark the future Bellemore Road. The very visible driveway in the distance leads to the Norton house, formerly the Duval house, just north of the intersection of Roland and Lake Avenues. It was built in 1882 and is now 800 West Lake Avenue. (Courtesy of BCPL.)

Looking south from Lake and Roland Avenues, S.A. Douglas took this image for the State Roads Commission on October 23, 1915. An insignificant Lake Avenue comes in from the left, just this side of the group of workmen. The northbound side of Roland Avenue is being paved. Its southbound carriageway is the muddy area to the left of the tracks. (Courtesy of Tony Pinto.)

After the conversion of the 29 trolley to bus service in 1947, the 24 streetcar from Upland Road to Lakeside continued to operate. Roland Avenue did not go beyond Lake Avenue, so the trolley was the only means of getting farther north. But when the 29 bus line was extended north to Lake Avenue, the trackage from Lake Avenue southward was removed. Only a short track, three-quarters of a mile, was left, from Lakeside to Lake Avenue, where it dead-ended (at left). With only one car running, there was no need for two tracks. The northbound track was taken up, and car 5687 ran up and down the southbound track from Lake Avenue to Lakeside for a couple of years (below). On January 28, 1950, car 5687 made its last run and was then dismantled and buried on the spot at the Lake Avenue end. (Both, courtesy of BSM.)

Car 5389 heads southward towards Lake Avenue, past Cochran's Pond. The Cochran's Pond stop and the Lakeside terminus existed to serve the houses on Woodbrook Lane, as well as originally to convey people to the now long-defunct Lake Side Park leisure park (closed in 1909) and the scenic Lake Roland area. This image was probably taken in 1946. (Courtesy of BSM.)

Car 5392 has left the Lakeside terminus and is heading toward Cochran's Pond. The photograph is dated June 15, 1947—meaning that the northbound track, on the right, will soon be torn up. Car 5392 and all others but one will be taken south into the city, with the rails taken up behind them. Only car 5687 will be left here on the rump bit of remaining trackage until January 1950. (Courtesy of BSM.)

Car 5687 heads north toward the Lakeside terminus, the shed visible through the trees to the right. The northbound track has been torn up. With only one car on one track, the turning loop has gone, too. Formerly, it curved to the left beyond the terminus shed and came back around to rejoin the main track. The loop's right-of-way is what looks like a dirt road coming in from the left. (Courtesy of BSM.)

Taken on November 3, 1946, this photograph shows car 5389 at the Lakeside terminus, the northernmost extremity of the No. 24 line. From this point, the cars turned to their left around the turning loop, which rejoined the southbound track 100 or so yards behind the car shown here. The house in the background is 205 Woodbrook Lane. (Courtesy of BSM.)

Five

SOUTHERN EPITOME

By 1910, the Roland Park Company had turned its attention south of Cold Spring Lane to Plats 4 and 5. The Olmsteds had been contemplating this area since 1905, but no action had been taken. Plans for Plat 5 were filed with the authorities in 1911, and those for Plat 4A in 1915. (Plat 4 was always called 4A.) This southern area presented various problems. A major one was cost. Mostly west of Roland Avenue, the very small Plat 4 extended from Cold Spring Lane south to the city line, while to the east about half of Plat 5 was in fact located within the city, whose boundary was an east/west line across University Parkway. Because the purchase of land so close to the city had been expensive, it was necessary develop more densely so as to create a greater number of sellable lots.

The result was a development characterized by formality and terraced roads, primarily running east/west, atop and along the slope that fell from the plateau south of Cold Spring Lane down to University Parkway. The development also featured townhomes and semidetached houses, almost unknown elsewhere in Roland Park. Another element of Plat 5 was the creation of two more fairly dense "communities within a community," a theme experimented with previously at Club Road, Goodwood Gardens, and Edgevale Park. With regard to the latter, the Plat 3 houses bounded by Englewood Road, Falls Road Terrace, and Edgevale Road enjoyed a shared private park in between them. The pattern was now replicated with the "Parkway triangle," bounded by University Parkway, Fortieth Street, and Cedar Avenue (now Keswick Road). These houses, too, were supposed to share a private communal park in the interior between them, though in fact this park did not materialize. Truer to the theme was Merryman Court, then called Northfield Court. The idea behind Merryman Court, where six houses surrounded a common green, was to suggest an old English close. There was only one entrance to the walled-off Merryman Court, which shielded the mini-development from the outside world. This theme was then repeated in Plat 4, though without the barrier wall.

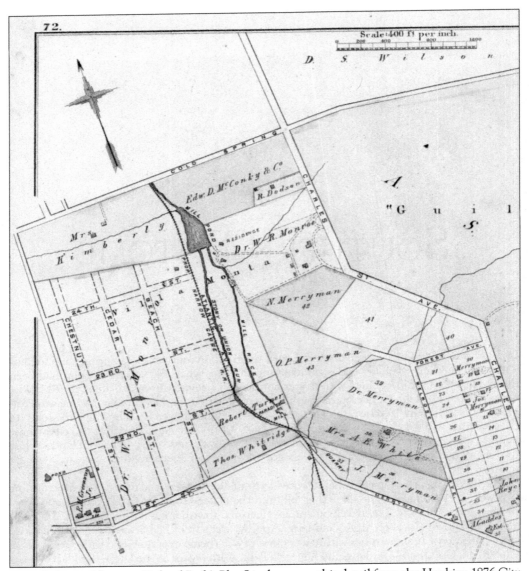

Part of what will become Roland Park's Plat 5 is shown on this detail from the Hopkins 1876 *City Atlas*. The platted area between Charles Street and Melrose Avenue is now Tuscany-Canterbury. Merryman's Lane is the precursor of University Parkway. The proposed subdividing of the Monroe estate into a row house–style street grid never occurred—though the very southern end of Roland Park, occupying the unshaded angle at the bottom center of the map, did end up grid patterned. What is shown as Twenty-first Street here is now Fortieth Street. The E.M. Greenway–owned houses on Twenty-first Street at the bottom left of the map are the three stone cottages on today's Fortieth Street that are now part of the Roland Park Place retirement community. The Kimberly estate, top left, is now the Keswick neighborhood. The millpond is gone, as is the millrace, which once flowed through the middle of today's Linkwood Park. (Courtesy of MSASC.)

This aerial photograph showing Plat 5 and beyond was probably taken in about 1924. Only one house on the north side of the 600 block of Fortieth Street has been constructed (No. 610, built in 1923), and none on the 4000 block of Cedar Avenue (now Keswick Road). Building on these blocks mostly occurred from 1925–1928. (Courtesy of Tony Pinto.)

Radically different from the grid pattern envisioned for this area on the 1876 map at the beginning of this chapter, Plat 5 as laid out by the Olmsteds consisted mostly of a series of east/west-oriented, curved streets cascading southward toward the then city boundary (bisecting University Parkway). This June 1911 view looks west from what is now Rugby Road. (Courtesy of Tony Pinto.)

This is the Roland Water Tower under construction in 1904. The tower in fact never provided water to Roland Park; it served Hampden, immediately south. The standpipe is still intact within the 148-foot tower built around it. It has a capacity of 211,000 gallons. The tower was designed in 1903 by William J. Fizone and was built in 1904–1905. (Courtesy of Tony Pinto.)

After the completion of the standpipe shown on the opposite page, this Beaux-Arts tower, pictured here in 1970, was built around it. This is one of only two such towers in Maryland, the other one being three miles west in West Arlington. Located on the southern boundary of Plat 4, the tower fell into disuse in 1930 when the City of Baltimore moved to using reservoirs exclusively for its water supply. (Courtesy of BCPL.)

In the 1943 image above, the streetcar is the 24 from Lakeside at the water tower. The trackless trolley is the No. 10. The 10 line had once been served by a tracked streetcar through Hampden, going as far north as Upland Road. In April 1940, the line was switched to trackless. Now, the northern turning point was the tower, as the Roland Park Civic League did not want trackless trolleys in Roland Park. The 24 streetcar had previously shuttled between Lakeside and Upland Road. As of 1940, it went south to the water tower to make the connection with the trackless No. 10. The image at left, taken on June 17, 1959, shows a 1942 Pullman trackless trolley at the tower loop. Trolleybuses were withdrawn in Baltimore four days later, June 21. (Above, courtesy of Tony Pinto; left, courtesy of BSM.)

The No. 24 streetcar pictured above has stopped on Roland Avenue at the water tower. It has just "changed ends" to head northward again. Streetcars had two trolley poles, though only one connected at a time to the power lines: the one at the opposite end from the direction of travel. "Changing ends" meant detaching the pole from the wire at one end of the car and raising the one at the other end, permitting the car to go back the way it came. This is well shown in the image below, where the car is heading toward the photographer—with the closer of the two poles lowered. The image above dates to between 1940 and 1947. The image below was taken on September 14, 1946, and shows a Union Avenue, Hampden jerkwater (minor route) shuttle using a No. 24 car. (Both, courtesy of BSM.)

Streetcars such as these two early 20th-century Brill vehicles had cabs at either end and could go in either direction. Above, southbound car 5389 has halted at the Roland Water Tower. Because this is a "stub-end track"—one with no turning loop—the motorman has stopped and will shortly "change ends" and "trim the car." This will entail lowering the pole closer to the photographer and raising the one farther away (permitting northbound travel), along with flipping the seatbacks and bringing the fare box to the cab at this end. Below, the end changing has occurred, and this car (a different one) is northbound past the water tower. Both photographs date to the period between 1940 and 1947. (Above, courtesy of BSM; below, courtesy of Leslie Goldsmith.)

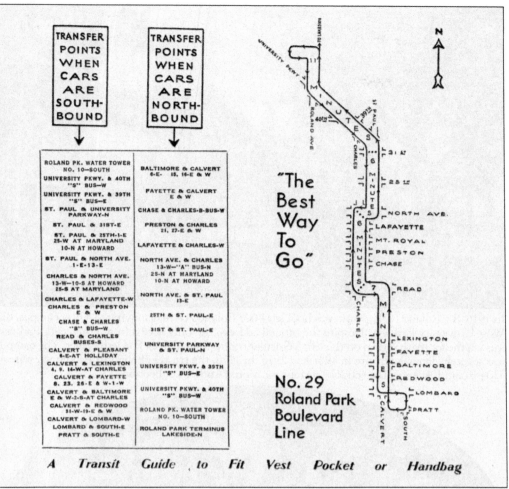

This is a route map for the No. 29 streetcar line from Calvert and Pratt Streets northward to the Upland Road car house in Roland Park, via University Parkway, as of March 1, 1939. The map claims a total route time of 30 minutes. (Courtesy of Leslie Goldsmith.)

In 1916, the Roland Park Country School left 4608 Roland Avenue, moving to a new campus, 817 West University Parkway. Despite the official address, the only access from University Parkway was via the footpath shown on the left. Vehicular traffic entered from Fortieth Street. The campus was severely damaged by fire in 1947 and 1976. In 1978, the trustees bought the Dohme estate at 5204 Roland Avenue, the school's current location. (Author's collection.)

The Daughters of Charity opened the Kirkleigh Villa retirement home for older women in 1926. It operated at 4301 Roland Avenue until 1966, when it was sold to the Society of Mary, a Catholic religious order. Bought by a developer in 2008, the building was demolished in October 2009 and replaced by a new memory-care facility, Symphony Manor. This photograph appears in a 1926 advertising brochure. (Author's collection.)

These photographs come from the same 1926 brochure as the second image on the opposite page. The photographer was standing at an upper window of the Kirkleigh building. The above view looks south toward the Roland Water Tower. As for the image below, the photographer is looking north toward Cold Spring Lane. The garden that dominates this image was developed in the 1960s as an apartment complex. On the opposite side of the road, the house farthest to the right—with five dormer windows, at the end of the row—was the residence that stood at the southwest corner of Roland Avenue and Cold Spring Lane. This house was demolished in the 1960s to permit the widening of Cold Spring Lane. (Both, author's collection.)

St. Mary's Female Orphan Asylum operated from 1818 to 1960, moving to this Roland Park location in 1886. The photographer of the image above is facing south in about 1900 at the orphanage's main entrance at 701 East Cold Spring Lane. The orphanage had a large patio behind it, seen in the undated photograph below. Judging by the clothing, this image also dates to around 1900. In the 20th century, the patio was roofed over. The orphanage was demolished to make way for the Roland Springs community of 104 townhouses, erected between 1974 and 1989. There is now not even a trace of the old orphanage. (Both, courtesy of Daughters of Charity.)

Six

COMMERCIAL BOUNDARY

Falls Road forms the western boundary of Roland Park and the approximate western edge of this book's coverage. Once an Indian trail, Falls Road led north from Baltimore and eventually extended all the way up to Pennsylvania. The first few miles parallel the Jones Falls River. First called Tyson's Mill Road, by 1807 it was the Falls Turnpike Road. There were initially tollhouses at North Avenue (the city boundary from 1815 to 1888), at Cross Keys Village (Falls Road and Cold Spring Lane), and a little south of Rockland Mills. The tollgate at Cross Keys stood near an old inn whose signboard bore two large, crossed keys. From this sign, the village took its name. In the late 1700s, free African Americans had settled in the village, seeking work in the nearby mills on the Jones Falls River. A century later, the village was home to about 500 people.

A little to the north, Cross Keys Village petered out, with both sides of Falls Road bordered by the Baltimore Country Club's 18-hole golf course (with fairways 1, 17, and 18 on the east side and the rest on the west side). North of the golf course, there was in the late 19th century little development along Falls Road until Washingtonville and Mount Washington. The Roches, whose descendants still live in the immediate area, owned a store at 5813 Falls Road. It was destroyed in the 1950s, and Joe's Bike Shop now occupies the site. A late-1990s attempt to develop 35–40 townhouses immediately east of Washingtonville under the name Fallslake aroused passionate opposition. A compromise instead saw 18 high-end single-family houses constructed as the Washingtonville Addition.

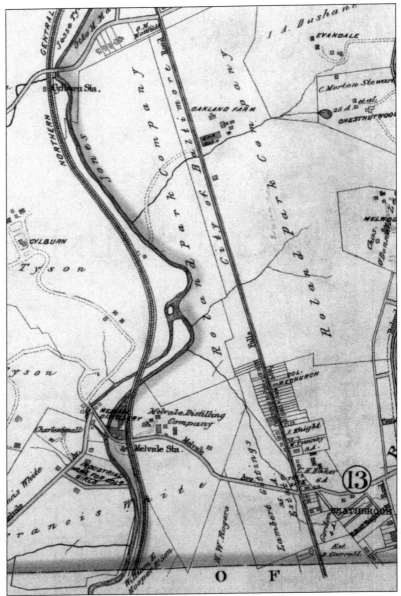

This detail from the 1898 Bromley *Atlas of Baltimore County* shows the lower half of Falls Road within the area under consideration, from the 1888 city line to Belvedere Avenue (now Northern Parkway). Cold Spring Lane west of Falls Road was called Melvale Avenue. The northern sections of the White and Gittings estates, above Melvale Avenue, are where the Baltimore Polytechnic Institute and Western High School now stand. The small developed area along Falls Road above Melvale Avenue but below the Roland Park Company holdings was called Cross Keys Village. Most of it was razed in the 1960s to make way for the Western High School parking lot, though a handful of the houses on the eastern side of Falls Road survived. Most of the vacant land shown here as being owned by the Roland Park Company ended up being the Baltimore Country Club's 18-hole golf course, with the exception of the area north of the Oakland Farm, which became part of Plat 6. The carbarn shown near the farm served the No. 25 trolley line. (Courtesy of MSASC.)

94

This map detail, from the same 1898 atlas as that on the opposite page, shows Falls Road from Belvedere Avenue to Lake Roland. The railroad on the left of the map is the Northern Central Railway, formerly the Baltimore & Susquehanna Railroad. The road branching to the left across the Jones Falls River from Falls Road, about a quarter of the way up the map, is Smith Avenue. At the time, this was the only road bridge to Mount Washington, the Kelly Avenue bridge at the time being solely used for streetcars. The Methodist Episcopal church (denoted "M.E. Ch.") marked on the map just below this is today the Mount Washington United Methodist Church. The lower Buchanan estate, southeast of the Jones Falls River, is now Lake Falls and Buckingham Manor. (Courtesy of MSASC.)

J.W. Schaefer took this photograph on October 6, 1910, for the State Roads Commission. He was looking north on Falls Road from a point about 50 yards south of Cold Spring Lane, the latter being the grade crossing in the middle distance. The typed caption on the back of the print reads, "View showing process of adapting tracks on account of the work of the State Roads Commission." (Courtesy of Tony Pinto.)

This early 20th-century photograph shows the view from the Gittings estate across Falls Road toward Ridgewood Road, on the crest. Just beyond the cows is Cross Keys Village, a community that had, over the decades, grown up around an inn. In 1961, the city bought 31 village houses for $197,370 and demolished them for the purposes of realigning Cold Spring Lane and providing a site for Western High School. (Courtesy of Tony Pinto.)

David F. Tufaro took this photograph showing the old tennis clubhouse at the Baltimore Country Club from Falls Road in 1997. The c. 1900 tennis building was briefly the home of the Mount Washington Cricket Club, which after its move from Mount Washington leased land from the Baltimore Country Club. The country club took over the building for tennis purposes in 1903. It was demolished on December 10, 2008. (Courtesy of David F. Tufaro.)

The Baltimore & Northern Railway car house—later the No. 25 streetcar line car house—was built in 1897, the year this photograph was taken. The carbarn was shut in 1936 and sold a decade later, after which point it was demolished to make way for an apartment building (5203 Falls Road) constructed by the same developer that built the Park Lin apartments on the site of the nearby Upland Road car house. (Courtesy of BCPL.)

Looking east along Belvedere Avenue—now Northern Parkway—from the southwest corner of Belvedere's intersection with Falls Road, an unidentified photographer took the image above. The box on the utility pole is the world's first sound-activated traffic signal, invented by Charles Adler Jr. Approaching cars sounded their horns, at which point the light would change in their favor. The device was installed at this location on February 22, 1928. The sign reads, "Stop. Sound horn to clear signal." One of Paul Dorsey's series of photographs of gasoline stations taken for Lightner Photography in the 1950s, the image below shows the same scene about three decades later. (Above, courtesy of BCPL; below, courtesy of BCPL/Lightner Photography.)

The photograph above was taken by Paul Dorsey the same day he took the lower image on the opposite page. The view is west along Belvedere Avenue toward the Belvedere Avenue Bridge, spanning the Jones Falls River and the Northern Central tracks, out of sight beyond the curve. The sign on the right reads, "Interstate Highway System. Interstate 83," implying that at least preliminary work on the Interstate 83 Jones Falls Expressway—paralleling the railroad—has already begun here. Ground was broken for the expressway on October 2, 1956. The photograph at right shows the Belvedere Avenue Bridge, viewed from the east by August H. Brinkmann in 1886, not long after its completion; Brinkmann was a Catonsville amateur photographer. (Above, courtesy of BCPL/Lightner Photography; right, courtesy of BCPL.)

The Belvedere Avenue Bridge is here seen from the southwest in 1908. The railroad tracks are those of the Northern Central. This right-of-way is now used by the Baltimore Light Rail, which in all but name represents a return to the streetcar era. The buildings in the distance are part of the Mount Washington Athletic Club. (Courtesy of BCPL.)

This May 1962 photograph, taken from the northeast, shows the demolition of the Belvedere Avenue bridge to make way for the Jones Falls Expressway and its associated interchanges. First approved by the Baltimore County commissioners on April 23, 1883, the old bridge served for 79 years. The expressway opened for traffic on November 2, 1962. (Courtesy of BCPL.)

This c. 1893 image shows pupils at Sally Welsh's school near Falls Road and Belvedere Avenue. Welsh herself is at the far right. The school sat more or less where the Shell service station now is at the northeast corner of the Falls Road and Northern Parkway intersection. (Courtesy of BCPL.)

This July 19, 1911, photograph was shot for the State Roads Commission by Edgar Schaefer. It shows work on the former Baltimore & Northern streetcar line. The back of the print reads, "Falls Road at Court McSherry." Court McSherry was Richard McSherry's Ciffhurst estate, shown on the second map at this chapter's start. The photographer is facing south on Falls Road, with Mattfeldt Avenue behind and to the right. (Courtesy of Tony Pinto.)

This late-1950s Paul Dorsey photograph taken for Lightner Photography shows the Scarff Auto Amoco station at Falls Road and Kelly Avenue. Somewhat altered, these buildings survive today as an auto mechanic facility, though without the fuel pumps. The building on the far left is now home to Joe's Bike Shop. (Courtesy of BCPL/ Lightner Photography.)

Taken sometime in the very early 20th century, this undated photograph shows the Mount Washington Light and Power Company's station on the northwest bank of the Jones Falls, immediately west of the Falls Road bridge over the river. This electricity-generating station supplied power for the streetlights in nearby Mount Washington. Today, on approximately this spot, there is a large Baltimore Gas and Electric Company substation. (Courtesy of BCPL.)

Seven

NORTHERN NEIGHBORS

None of the areas covered in this chapter is actually within Roland Park proper. Nonetheless, their history is entwined with that of Roland Park, for Roland Park's success paved the way for theirs.

New North Roland Park and Poplar Hill, north of Northern Parkway and mostly west of Roland Avenue, are considered to be a single neighborhood today. Their early development was, broadly speaking, contemporary with Roland Park's. This is to say that certain estate houses in the area predate Roland Park and are still existent, while others were built just after Roland Park and were intended for sale to similar clientele. Indeed, some North Roland Parkers were former Roland Parkers who wanted larger lots or larger houses. (Some of New North Roland Park/Poplar Hill is less densely developed than Roland Park.) An example is the Tottle family, featured in this chapter, who in 1912 moved from Roland Park's Plat 3 to a small estate called Sunset Knoll in North Roland Park, once part of the old Lehr estate. The former Lehr estate was the southwestern anchor of New North Roland Park.

Another Roland Park Company project, to the immediate east, is the Orchards, a community of 127 houses dating to the 1930s and developed on the Gordon estate between Charles Street and Roland Avenue. The Gordon house still exists within the Orchards, as do various outbuildings now part of the Bryn Mawr School, which bought part of the Gordon estate in 1928, subsequently moving there from its former home downtown.

The Orchards and New North Roland Park/Poplar Hill extend as far north as Lake Avenue. Just beyond this road are a number of small, post–World War II neighborhoods, interspersed with a few older houses. These are wedged between Lake Avenue and Lake Roland, the 1861 municipal reservoir (originally called Swann Lake). The oldest of these postwar developments, the Village of Lake Falls (1948), is covered extensively at the end of this chapter.

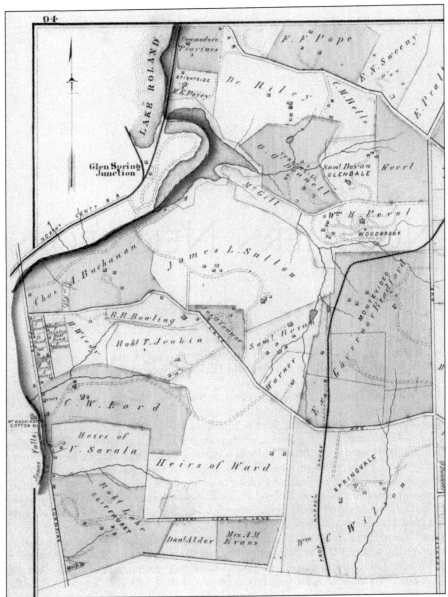

This detail from the Hopkins 1876 *City Atlas* shows the area that will one day become Roland Park's neighboring developments to the north. The Wilson estate, at bottom right, will eventually become the Orchards. The Alder, Evans, Lehr, and Ward estates will make up the heart of New North Roland Park/Poplar Hill. The Bradfords' Montevideo estate is now the Elkridge Club, while the Bevan land is today's Boys' Latin School. The old Sutton holdings make up the general Lakehurst area. The Buchanan estate, farthest to the left, is now developed as Lake Falls Village and Buckingham Manor. Toward the top of the map, what is labeled as the "Glen Spring Junction" should actually be Green Spring Junction." The line to the left (northwest) is the Greenspring branch of the Northern Central Railway, which was also used by the Western Maryland Railroad to connect trains to its station at Owings Mills. The main Northern Central line continues northward from the junction. (Courtesy of MSASC.)

The John W. and Helen Doll Tottle family, introduced in chapter three while they were still living in Plat 3, moved to Sunset Knoll (shown above as it appeared in the 1960s) in 1912. At the western end of Lehr Lane (now St. George's Road), the Southern plantation–style house had been built for them while they were renting on Longwood Road. John Tottle was a well-to-do merchant, having made good with a successful chain of local five-and-dime stores, such as the Lexington Street one shown in the turn-of-the-20th-century postcard below. (Both, courtesy of Barrie Sigler.)

Lexington Street (Shopping District), Baltimore, Md.

This c. 1913 photograph shows Tottle daughters Anna Doll (left) and Helen on the Sunset Knoll driveway, with the photographer looking northeast. The dirt road atop the ridge in the background is Lehr Lane, while the road sloping down to the right beyond the tall grass is the nameless lane connecting Lehr Lane (St. George's Road) to Belvedere Avenue (Northern Parkway). (Courtesy of Barrie Sigler.)

These children are Sandra Frey and Dick Allen, grandchildren of John and Helen Tottle by, respectively, daughters Florence and Anna Doll. Immediately behind them are the Sunset Knoll tennis courts. The light-colored building through the trees is a garage, added in the late 1920s or early 1930s. Beyond the garage is the house itself. This photograph was probably taken in 1936. (Courtesy of Barrie Sigler.)

Pictured in about 1913 on Sunset Knoll's side porch are, from left to right, Anna Doll, Helen, and John Jr.—the three eldest Tottle children. The view is to the east. The unpaved road sloping down from left to right is Belvedere Avenue, now Northern Parkway, and the house in the distance is what is now 902 West Northern Parkway, built in 1912. (Courtesy of Barrie Sigler.)

This photograph, of the same vintage as the one above, shows the view west from Sunset Knoll. The structures visible are the outbuildings of the Dixons' Cliffhurst estate. Shown on the map at the beginning of this chapter as the Lehr estate, the land was sold in 1888 to Richard M. McSherry. The McSherrys in 1900 divided the 43-acre tract, selling the southern 25 acres to Isaac H. Dixon. (Courtesy of Barrie Sigler.)

This image shows Helen Doll Tottle with her four eldest children, from left to right, John Jr., Florence, Anna Doll, and Helen. Doll was Helen Tottle's maiden name, and third child Anna always went by "Anna Doll." The location of this shot is unknown; the year is probably 1914 or 1915. (Courtesy of Barrie Sigler.)

The image at left shows John W. Tottle in his later years, on his birthday in May 1944, surrounded mostly by grandchildren in the dining room at Sunset Knoll. The woman at the back, holding the baby, is daughter Helen, the child farthest to the right in the previous image on this page. (Courtesy of Barrie Sigler.)

This is a Tottle family gathering at Sunset Knoll in 1967. Tottle daughters Anna Doll, Elizabeth, and Helen are, respectively, first (floral dress), third (seated, with back turned), and fifth (wearing glasses and reading) from the left. By this time, the family was long out of the retail business, having sold the store company to the Pittsburgh-based G.C. Murphy five-and-dime chain in the 1920s. (Courtesy of Barrie Sigler.)

The Order of the Visitation of Holy Mary was founded in 1610 in France. In 1833, the order established its first convent in America, in the District of Columbia. A Baltimore convent followed in 1837, the original Baltimore location being at Green and Mulberry Streets. The order moved its Baltimore establishment to 5712 Roland Avenue in New North Roland Park on June 16, 1927, about the time this postcard was made. (Author's collection.)

This is Michael Jenkins's Woodglen house at 822 West Lake Avenue, a property previously owned by Samuel Bevan. The photograph is undated but probably goes back to the early 20th century. The scene shows a group preparing for a fox hunt, perhaps at the neighboring Elkridge Fox Hunting Club (now a country club). The old Jenkins house is now the Boys' Latin Upper School main building, Williams Hall. (Courtesy of BCPL.)

The Elkridge Club, originally a foxhunting club, is housed on the former Augustus W. Bradford estate. (Bradford was Maryland's governor during the Civil War.) In 1888, the 10-year-old club leased 54 acres from the estate; it bought most of this acreage in 1892. Some of the hunting land was turned into a nine-hole golf course in 1895. The view in this photograph, taken in 1906, is looking northward from the tennis courts. (Courtesy of BCPL.)

Dam & Pumphouse Lake Roland.

The image above shows the 40-foot-high dam at Lake Roland in 1886. The one at right shows the same scene in early 1955. James Slade of Hartford, Connecticut, was the dam's designer, and Charles P. Manning was its construction supervisor. While Lake Roland is situated in Baltimore County, it is owned by the City of Baltimore, which developed the dam and the 100-acre lake behind it in the late 1850s as a water supply. The city bought the water rights in 1857 for $289,000; the entire cost of the project was $1,360,057. The lake fed water into an underground conduit that carried it about four miles south to the Hampden reservoir (now filled in). The lake functioned as a water supply only until 1915, when its usage was discontinued because of siltation. (Above, courtesy of BCPL; right, courtesy of the Clark family.)

Lake Roland Bridge.

This image shows the bridge just downstream from Lake Roland from which countless photographs of the dam have been taken. August Brinkmann took this photograph in 1886. This is a Wendel Bollman truss bridge, built in 1872. Bollman was a mid-19th-century self-taught civil engineer. This bridge was replaced in 1952, and again in 2010. (Courtesy of BCPL.)

LAKE ROLAND DAM, ROLAND PARK, BALTIMORE, MD.

A c. 1920 postcard shows the Lake Roland dam from the rear. The lake is primarily fed by the Jones Falls River and Roland Run. The building on the opposite (southeast) bank is the valve house, where the controls to the dam's sluices are located. (Author's collection.)

To take the 1886 image above, Catonsville photographer August Brinkmann probably stood at the northeastern end of the stone pier that surrounds the Lake Roland dam valve house. The shot is of the opposite (northwest) bank, which forms part of Relay Hill. The photograph below shows approximately the same view in 1956, taken from about 150 yards upstream. Note how denuded of trees the 165-yard-wide peninsula was in the 1950s. These days, its entire perimeter is tree covered (even if the middle is not), such that a replication of this scene today would look more like the 1886 shot than the 1956 one. Relay Hill has been used as a recreational area since the lake was first created. (Above, courtesy of BCPL; below, courtesy of the Clark family.)

This 1886 Brinkmann image is of the Northern Central Railway causeway and bridge across Lake Roland, immediately north of Green Spring Junction. The white building at the far left is the junction's Hollins Station. The station was closed for reasons of economy in 1928; it burned down in 1933. Its remnants may still be found in the underbrush. (Courtesy of BCPL.)

Lake Roland.

The Lake Station was seven-tenths of a mile north of Hollins Station, just south of Rolandvue Road. The stop served area residents until 1959, when the Northern Central eliminated passenger service. Freight service continued until 1972, when the company went under. The image dates to 1958. This scene is no longer replicable because this northern end of the lake is now silted over and partially forested. (Courtesy of BCPL.)

This photograph shows Estelle B. and husband Charles A. LaPointe on Lake Falls Road on Easter Day, 1951. Estelle was known as "Jerrie," and Charles as "Al." They were stalwarts of Lake Falls Village for decades. All of Lake Falls Road, plus the even-numbered (northern) side of the 1200 block of West Lake Avenue, along with small parts of the 1100 and 1300 blocks of West Lake, make up the Village of Lake Falls. Lake Falls is built on the western half of what at the beginning of this chapter is shown on the map as the Buchanan estate. It comprises 40 houses, completed between 1948 and 1951. The Lake Falls Construction Company bought the land (11.65 acres) in 1947 for $16,500. Moving into 1205 Lake Falls Road in late spring 1948, the LaPointes were the development's second residents, their close friends Frederick W. and Doris H. Gould having already moved into 1210 Lake Falls Road on May 1. (Courtesy of the Clark family.)

This December 1947 photograph shows Jerrie LaPointe standing at the front door of the unfinished 1205 Lake Falls Road. Capitalizing on the postwar housing boom, Lake Falls was intended to provide comparatively low-cost housing for Baltimore's new middle class, especially returning war veterans. Such buyers had previously had only limited access to the suburban lifestyle due to the high cost of places such as Roland Park. (Courtesy of the Clark family.)

The LaPointes took this photograph of their house-to-be in November 1947. Built for budget-conscious buyers, the Lake Falls houses came in only four basic patterns: the A, B, C, and D styles, along with a single Cape Cod. However, each style had variations, so the neighborhood is not as "cookie-cutter" as one might suppose. (Courtesy of the Clark family.)

This March 1954 LaPointe photograph shows how 1205 Lake Falls Road looked once completed. The garage-top patio was for years a favorite gathering place for the gregarious LaPointes and their friends. Unable to have children, the LaPointes were great entertainers. In later years, the patio had a two-floor addition built on it, increasing the size of the house by about a quarter. (Courtesy of the Clark family.)

Taken in March 1949, this is the view west from the LaPointes' backyard. The houses immediately beyond the fence are 1209 (right) and 1211 Lake Falls Road. They are, respectively, C2- and B1-style houses. The open land beyond and to the left of 1211 is the much-loved Breezeway, a small park in the middle of Lake Falls. (Courtesy of the Clark family.)

The jewel in the Lake Falls crown is the Breezeway, the open space in the middle of this 1954 shot. The 1.2-acre community park bisects the neighborhood. The reason it was never developed is that under it is a conduit that once carried water from Lake Roland to Hampden. A developer attempted to build on the Breezeway in 2003–2004, but strenuous community opposition put paid to the plan. (Courtesy of the Clark family.)

This photograph dates to early 1954. In the middle is 1210 Lake Falls Road, a C1-style house and home of the LaPointes' friends the Goulds. In the late 1950s, an addition was put on the east (right) side of the house, with the front door relocated to the addition. The house on the left, 1212, is a B2 house, one of the last to be completed. (Courtesy of the Clark family.)

This is "Aunt Jerrie" LaPointe on the front pathway of 1210 Lake Falls Road, the Goulds' house. The baby is Byrant, the Goulds' first child, on his christening day in 1950. The doorway in the background is now a window, the front door having been moved to an addition built on the right side of the house in the late 1950s. (Courtesy of the Clark family.)

These two photographs were taken at the same cookout, probably in 1954, in the Goulds' backyard. In the picture at left, hosts Fred and Doris Gould are, respectively, at the far left and far right. The white-haired older man is "Pops" Gould, Fred's father. The house in the background of the left picture is 1210 Lake Falls Road, the Goulds' home. The garage, with its rooftop screened-in porch, was added by the Goulds in the early 1950s; subsequently, they would add another extension on the east (left) side of the house. The house in the background of the photograph below is next-door 1208, owned by J. Lawrence Lears, vice president of the Lake Falls Construction Company. (Both, courtesy of the Clark family.)

The photograph above shows Christmas 1953 in the Goulds' living room at 1210 Lake Falls Road. Doris Gould is the clown, while husband Fred is Santa Claus. Three-year-old son Bryant looks on expectantly, while little sister Ellen, nearly two, crawls toward the goody sacks. The image below was taken on the occasion of Ellen's fourth birthday party, January 1956, in the basement of 1210. Ellen is third from the right. Her mother, Doris, is by the Christmas tree. Fred and Doris were Lake Falls' first residents, but they were not alone long. Advertising for the new development was largely by word of mouth, and sales were brisk. Many of the original residents had known each other previously. (Both, courtesy of the Clark family.)

The St. Joseph's Day blizzard of March 19, 1958, brought two feet of snow to Baltimore. This is Jerrie LaPointe surveying the aftermath. The houses behind Jerrie are, from left, 1212, 1210, and 1208 Lake Falls Road. (Courtesy of the Clark family.)

Jerrie LaPointe (middle) and Ginny Seims are on the front lawn of 1207 Lake Falls Road with local children in July 1958. Ginny's children, Bobby and Porter, are, respectively, top left and bottom right. The Goulds' son Bryant is between the women. The three girls with short, dark hair and striped T-shirts are Lake Falls builder Larry Leers's daughters, Mary Kate, Louise, and Maggie (left to right). The girls between Mary Kate and Louise are Molly Chittenden (white shirt) and Clairy Henkle. The baby in the playpen is Lovey Henkle. (Courtesy of the Clark family.)

The LaPointes were car aficionados, with a soft spot for Chryslers. This is a 1950 Chrysler Newport, bought that year and parked out front. The lawn in the foreground looks lush; it was not always so. When initially sold, the Lake Falls houses had bare clay dirt yards. Buyers wishing for an immediate lawn had to pay extra for sodding. The house in the background is 1206 Lake Falls. (Courtesy of the Clark family.)

The hip-roofed 1206 Lake Falls Road is featured in this photograph, too, with 1204 and 1202 beyond it. The teenager in the middle is Ellen Gould, daughter of the Goulds at 1210 Lake Falls Road, across whose flagstone pathway Ellen has just run. The image probably dates to the late 1960s. (Courtesy of the Clark family.)

The majority of the Lake Falls houses are of standard clapboard construction with a brick veneer. However, the D- and B2-style houses (the latter shown here) came with fairly unusual board-and-batten siding. (The battens are the thin wooden strips between the wide boards.) The Thorntons are shown having just cleared snow from in front of their house, 1216 Lake Falls Road, in January 1955. (Courtesy of the Clark family.)

Pictured here are 1206 (left) and 1208 West Lake Avenue as seen from 1205 Lake Falls Road. This is January 1955. Like the overwhelming majority of Lake Falls houses, these two have since been considerably expanded. Built on fairly generous lots—the largest is just shy of half an acre—the Lake Falls houses had room to grow. Nearly all have had additions put on, sometimes nearly doubling the original size. (Courtesy of the Clark family.)

With its Breezeway community park and with Lake Roland nearby, Lake Falls is a children's neighborhood. (This is enhanced by the fact that Lake Falls Road, graded in 1947, was Baltimore County's last narrow, 24-foot-wide road, forcing drivers to proceed at a snail's pace, to the delight of street-playing kids.) These images show Santa's visit to Lake Falls on December 17, 1955. The "horseless sleigh" has been parked on the Breezeway, seen at right, and gifts are being distributed. The image below shows people packing up after the Santa excitement. The woman in the middle is Julia Klingenstein, who, along with her husband, John, lived at 1228 Lake Falls Road. The house in the immediate background is 1211 Lake Falls Road. (Both, courtesy of the Clark family.)

Breezeway gatherings among Lake Falls residents are frequent. This photograph is of the 1976 Fourth of July get-together. The house in the background, visible through the trees, is 1208 West Lake Avenue. Pictured among the crowd is the woman who is now Lake Falls' longest-term resident. In the back row, toward the left, is a man in an Uncle Sam top hat. Two people to the right and one in front is a woman with short, dark hair holding a paper cup. This is Barbara Taylor, who moved to Lake Falls Road in September 1948. Now in her 90s, she is Lake Falls' sole remaining original resident. The "Lake Falls" banner, made by the late Ellen Parsons, is still very much in evidence at Breezeway events. (Courtesy of Roy Parsons.)

BIBLIOGRAPHY

Baltimore Country Club. *Baltimore Country Club: One Hundred Years*. Baltimore: Baltimore Country Club, 1998.

Hilton, George W. *The Ma & Pa: A History of the Maryland & Pennsylvania Railroad*. 2nd ed. La Jolla, CA: Howell-North Books, 1980.

Kelly, Jacques. "JFX is a Long Stretch of History." *Baltimore Sun*, February 7, 2009.

Kolchak, Jim. *Baltimore's Two Cross Keys Villages: One Black, One White*. New York: iUniverse, Inc., 2004.

Lewand, Karen. *North Baltimore: From Estate to Development*. Baltimore: Baltimore City Department of Planning, 1989.

Moundry, Roberta M. "Gardens, Houses and People: The Planning of Roland Park, Baltimore." Master's thesis, Cornell University, 1990.

Simmons, George B. 1912. *A Book of Pictures in Roland Park, Baltimore, Maryland*. Baltimore: self-published, 1912.

Van Horn, Martin K., and Robert L. Williams. *Green Spring Accommodation: 130 Years of Railway History in the Green Spring Valley, Baltimore County, Maryland, 1832–1962*. Polo, IL: Transportation Trails, 1996.

Waesche, James F. *Crowning the Gravelly Hill: A History of the Roland Park—Guilford—Homeland District*. Baltimore: Maclay & Associates, 1987.

Visit us at
arcadiapublishing.com

CPSIA information can be obtained
at www.ICGtesting.com
Printed in the USA
LVOW02*0038070417
529950LV00009B/22/P